BAHÁ'Í EDUCATION FOR CHILDREN

Book 1

(A Teacher's Guide)

This book is to be used for
children of 5 to 6 years old

BAHÁ'Í EDUCATION FOR CHILDREN

BOOK – 1

(A Teacher's Guide)

A. A. Furútan

Bahá'í Publishing Trust
New Delhi, India

First Edition: December 1999
Reprint June 2000

ISBN: 81-86953-66-3

Published by the Bahá'í Publishing Trust
F 3/6, Okhla Industrial Area, Phase-I
New Delhi, India

Cover design: Shahla Mojanadi

Printed at Mercury Printer and Publisher, New Delhi

CONTENTS

v

FOREWORD

Bahá'í education for children is one of the most important lines of action for the consolidation of the Bahá'í communities. Through children's education, the whole community can gradually be transformed. Observing the great need for a systematic approach to this task, some 50 years ago Hand of the Cause of God 'Alí-Akbar Furútan developed a set of 13 books for the Bahá'í education of children. The books were written in the Persian language for use in the Bahá'í communities in Irán (Persia) and were known as the *Kitáb-i-Dars-i-Akhlagh* (*Books for Moral Education*). The set included 12 books for children aged 5 to 16-18 and a *Teacher's Manual* on the principles of Bahá'í education.

An administrative system was put in place by the National Spiritual Assembly of the Bahá'ís of Irán to assist generations of Bahá'í children to attend these classes, first as students, and later on in their youth and adulthood, as teachers. Availability of these materials the efforts of various institutions of the Faith and parents to systematically follow up the progress and assist Bahá'í communities to hold children's classes made children's education a vital activity in almost every Bahá'í community in Iran.

Inspired by the spirit of the four year plan and the need for the systematisation of human resource development, a group of Bahá'í friends in Zambia decided to translate these books into English for possible use by interested national communities. It was obvious from the outset that the books needed not only to be translated but adapted in many instances. With the full permission of Mr. Furútan, the adaptation and changes made in the books include information on the update of the progress of the Faith, modifications based on cultural considerations and the addition of new topics. We are very grateful to Mr. Furútan for his kind permission to make these changes.

We are also thankful to the friends who translated the books for their interest and hard work. May their meritorious service be crowned with the Bounty of the acceptance of the Blessed Beauty.

National Spiritual Assembly of the Bahá'ís of Zambia
Lusaka, June 1998

INTRODUCTION

This book contains a selection from the Bahá'í Writings on children's education. Teachers should study them and do their best to teach the children in accordance with the divine guidance. When children receive effective Bahá'í training at a young and tender age, they will be helped to grow up to be better Bahá'ís and an ornament to the world of humanity.

Here are some selections from the Bahá'í Writings on children's education:

> **Children must first be trained in divine virtues and encouraged and urged to improve their character. Thereafter, efforts must be made to teach them sciences, crafts and knowledge to the extent possible, for without heavenly virtues and upright character, the mere acquisition of learning and arts will not suffice.**[iii]
>
> **Good behaviour and high moral character must come first, for unless the character be trained, acquiring knowledge will only prove injurious. Knowledge is praiseworthy when it is coupled with ethical conduct and virtuous character; otherwise it is a deadly poison, a frightful danger.**[iv]
>
> **Let the mothers consider that whatever concerneth the education of children is of the first importance. Let them put forth every effort in this regard, for when the bough is green and tender it will grow in whatever way ye train it. Therefore it is incumbent upon the mothers to rear their little ones even as a gardener tendeth his young plants. Let them strive by day and by night to establish within their children faith and certitude, the fear of God, the love of the Beloved of the worlds, and all good qualities and**

traits. Whensoever a mother seeth that her child hath done well, let her praise and applaud him and cheer his heart; and if the slightest undesirable trait should manifest itself, let her counsel the child and punish him, and use means based on reason, even a slight verbal chastisement should this be necessary. It is not, however, permissible to strike a child, or vilify him, for the child's character will be totally perverted if he be subjected to blows or verbal abuse.[v]

Bring them [the children] up to work and strive, and accustom them to hardship.[vi]

If a plant is carefully nurtured by a gardener, it will become good, and produce better fruit. These children must be given a good training from their earliest childhood. They must be given a systematic training which will further their development from day to day, in order that they may receive greater insight, so that their spiritual receptivity be broadened. Beginning in childhood they must receive instruction. They cannot be taught through books. Many elementary sciences must be made clear to them in the nursery; they must learn them in play, in amusement. Most ideas must be taught them through speech, not by book learning. One child must question the other concerning these things, and the other child must give the answer. In this way, they will make great progress.... Later on, the children will of their own accord speak with each other concerning these same subjects.... They must be encouraged and when any one of them shows good advancement, for the further development they must be praised and encouraged therein. Even so in Godlike affairs.[vii]

The mother is the first teacher of the child. For children, at the beginning of life, are fresh and tender as a young twig, and can be trained in any fashion you desire. If you rear the child to be straight, he will

x

grow straight, in perfect symmetry. It is clear that the mother is the first teacher and that it is she who establisheth the character and conduct of the child.

Wherefore, O ye loving mothers, know ye that in God's sight, the best of all ways to worship Him is to educate the children and train them in all the perfections of humankind; and no nobler deed than this can be imagined."[viii]

As to the children: From the age of five their formal education must begin. That is, during the daytime they should be looked after in a place where there are teachers, and should learn good conduct.

Here they should be taught, in play, some letters and words and a little reading - as it is done in certain countries where they fashion letters and words out of sweets and give them to the child. For example, they make an "a" out of candy and say its name is "a", or make a candy "b" and call it "b", and so on with the rest of the alphabet, giving these to the young child. In this way, children will soon learn their letters... [ix]

If we want our children to have Bahá'í virtues and to be useful members of society, as teachers and parents we need to follow 'Abdu'l-Bahá's instructions on how to rear our children.

For more effective learning, teachers are encouraged to modify some details of the lessons (i.e. names, mention of climatic indicators, etc.) in a way that is appropriate for the culture of the children. Presentation of the subjects and the way discussions are encouraged can also be modified when thought necessary, using this book as a guideline. It is important, however, that when changes are made the spirit of the lessons and the messages to be conveyed are not changed.

Please note that some of the points in this book are given to the young children as instructions to be obeyed, without giving many reasons as to why they should be followed. While reasons can and should be given when possible, it is also necessary to explain that there are some laws which should be obeyed without much questioning. This is important when talking about instructions from a source of authority, especially from the Manifestation of God. With repetition and perseverance, children will learn obedience and see these instructions as habits they have to form in their lives. This is why, at this stage, little emphasis is given to the reasons for following the teachings of Bahá'u'lláh.

To ensure that the participants in children's classes, which are held in rural areas, have access to certain items, it would be of great value if a pocket were inserted in the inside cover of this book, containing the following:

- 3 photographs of 'Abdu'l-Bahá, including one of Him smiling, and another of Him with children
- 2 photographs of Shoghi Effendi
- 5 postcards showing the diversity of the Bahá'í community

It is also suggested that National Assemblies adopting the book may improve it by including some artwork representing the local culture of the country.

A. A. Furútan

---

[i] **'Abdu'l-Bahá**, *Bahá'í Education*, published in *The Compilation of Compilations*, Vol. 1, p. 280

[ii] **'Abdu'l-Bahá**, *Bahá'í Education*, published in *The Compilation of Compilations*, Vol. 1, p. 280

[iii] **'Abdu'l-Bahá**, *Authorised Translation*

[iv] **'Abdu'l-Bahá**, *Bahá'í Education*, published in *The Compilation of Compilations*, Vol. 1, p. 278

[v] **'Abdu'l-Bahá**, *Selections from the Writings of 'Abdu'l-Bahá*, p. 125

[vi] **'Abdu'l-Bahá**, *Selections from the Writings of 'Abdu'l-Bahá*, p. 129

[vii] **'Abdu'l-Bahá**, *Bahá'í Education*, published in *The Compilation of Compilations*, Vol. 1, p. 310

[viii] **'Abdu'l-Bahá**, *Bahá'í Education*, published in *The Compilation of Compilations*, Vol. 1, p. 288

[ix] **'Abdu'l-Bahá**, *Bahá'í Education*, published in *The Compilation of Compilations*, Vol. 1, p. 280

FORMAT OF A TYPICAL LESSON

Each day, the children's lesson will follow basically the same format. It is helpful for children to be in a structured and familiar environment. They will soon learn the format of the class and will look forward to each part of it. The class will begin with prayers. Then the teacher and children will review what was learned in the previous class. There is a brief break after the review, which includes activities such as singing, playing games, and an opportunity for the teacher to register the students. Following the break, the new lesson will be presented, usually with a brief explanation, a story, and sometimes a quotation or prayer to learn and memorise. If the teacher is able to get materials for the children to use, they may then draw and colour pictures related to the lesson. The class will close with a prayer, and then a final suggestion from the teacher, asking the children to do something specific at home. Below is a more detailed description of each of section of the class.

1. Opening prayer - Each lesson should begin with an opening prayer. One of the students or the teacher may say an opening prayer to start the lesson. If more than one student would like to say a prayer, this would also be acceptable, as it is good to encourage the children to do this. If they all know the same prayer, however, this is not the time for each of them to recite it. That can be done later as a class activity.

2. Review of previous lesson - Except for the first two lessons, each lesson will begin by reviewing what was learned in the previous class. The teacher can ask questions to give the children a chance to recall what they learned.

3. Break: songs, games, student registration and children's cleanliness - After the review, the children will enjoy singing and learning new songs and playing games.

Songs - Children should be encouraged to learn Bahá'í songs. If the teacher knows how to play a guitar or a local musical instrument, this will add to the joyful atmosphere of the class. Members of the community who play musical instruments may also be invited to play for the children.

Games - If the location and the environment are suitable for simple games, the teacher may play with the children. This will also prevent them from becoming bored. Games are already included with each lesson in these materials. Of course, if there is another game, which the children enjoy, you should feel free to use it. Choose games that are suitable to the children's age and the environment, to be played under the supervision of the teacher. If the environment is not suitable for this purpose, the children are asked to have a break and rest, with the teacher lovingly, patiently and firmly ensuring that they maintain acceptable behaviour.

The teacher may relay stories to the children. The teacher should try to tell the children, whenever appropriate, interesting stories with positive and spiritual morals. Other members of the community can also be invited to the class for the same purpose. Tapes of interesting stories can be played at times.

Student registration - The teacher should take advantage of the break time to register the students in a notebook, specially prepared and maintained for this purpose. The teacher may ask the children to listen for their names. When the teacher calls the child's name, the child can stand up to show that he/she is present. When the teacher notices that a student has missed more than one or two sessions, may inquire the reason from the student's parents or others, and help, if possible, to encourage the student to attend regularly.

Children's cleanliness - Another objective of the break time is for the teacher to see if all the students have paid sufficient attention to being clean. Of course, this must be done with utmost love, kindliness and patience, and without any student feeling in the slightest way that he/she is being inspected for cleanliness. The teacher tries to get close to the children to see if any one of them has neglected this important matter. Should it be necessary, and without addressing any one given child, the teacher may initiate a discussion when it is explained to them the importance of cleanliness and the disadvantages of uncleanness.

4. New lesson / story / memorisation - This is the new material presented during the lesson. It may be a story that the teacher tells to the children, or a prayer for the children to memorise. There is even a lesson where the children will learn a play during this part of class. Remember that stories should be told in ways that make it interesting to the children. The teacher should learn the story before telling it.

5. Drawing and colouring pictures (if material available) - Children enjoy drawing and colouring and this should be encouraged whenever possible. A picture is included with each lesson of the course. The teacher may get paper and colouring materials, and trace the pictures for the children to colour. This might be possible with the assistance of the parents and the Bahá'í community, who may be able to contribute such items, or help raise funds to buy them.

6. Closing prayer - Each class will end with a closing prayer. It is good to encourage the children to say a prayer. However, if none of them knows one, the teacher may say it. The teacher should lovingly remind the children how to behave when prayers are being said. They should be still and listen quietly and attentively.

7. Teacher's suggestion for the week - Before the children leave, the teacher will remind them of what they have learned, and will ask them to do something at home. The teacher may ask them to simply think about what they learned, or to tell the story from class to their family, or to practice the prayer they are memorising, or practice being clean, etc.

IN THE NAME OF GOD, THE MOST GLORIOUS

1. Getting to know the children
Bahá'í greeting: Alláh-u-Abhá

"Alláh-u-Abhá class."

1.1 Opening Prayer
One of the students or the teacher can say a prayer to start the lesson.

1.2 Introduction
When all the children, boys and girls, have gathered together, the teacher may begin talking to them as follows, to help them to get to know each other better:

"My dear children, my name is … and I am happy to be your teacher. Throughout the year, I would like to help you learn many things. You will come at least once a week to this class. You will learn things. You will play. You will sing songs. I will tell you stories. I will show you photographs. I am sure you will learn a lot and will also have a happy and enjoyable time when you come to this class.

"Today, we want to get to know each other better, learn each other's names and become friends. I have this notebook in front of me in which I am going to write your names. I will now ask each one of you to tell me your name."

The teacher calls one of the students and asks: "What is your name? What is your father's name? What is your mother's name? What is your family name?", and so on. The teacher registers the names of all the students in his/her notebook. "My dear children, I have registered all your names in my notebook. Now I will call you one by one. As you hear your name, please stand up for everyone to see you." The teacher calls all the names and each student stands up.

1.3 Games and Songs

Game: "Getting to Know Each Other"
"I also have a game that will help you remember each other's names. Please stand up and form a circle." The teacher helps the children to form a circle. "Wonderful! Now when I call your name, please go to the next child whose name I mention and shake his/her hand and say, 'Alláh-u-Abhá.' Please be attentive and let us start the game." The teacher begins the game, and ends it before the children show signs of boredom.

Other games to help children learn each other's names can also be used, such as the game Tutti Frutti.

Game: "Tutti Frutti"
Everyone sits in a circle. The teacher asks what are two fruits commonly known to everyone (for example, mangos and bananas). Whenever the teacher points to someone and says "mango", the person has to say the name of the individual on his/her left. When the teacher points to someone and says "banana", the person has to say the name of the person on his/her right. When the leader says "Tutti Frutti", everyone changes seats in a random manner. The game continues until the teacher feels everyone knows everyone else's name and before the children become bored.
"Now, dear children, we know each other a little bit better and we will get to know one another even more in the weeks to come. That is enough for today."

Song:
Teach the children the following song. (Also include some songs they already know.)

People of Bahá

We are people of Bahá (x2)
We are people of (x2)
We are people of Bahá.

Tuli anthu akwa Bahá (x2)
Tuli anthu akwa (x2)
Tuli anthu akwa Bahá.

We are teachers…
We are singers…
We are the children…

1.4 Bahá'í Greeting: 'Alláh-u-Abhá'

"Dear children, we are all Bahá'ís. Many of your parents are also Bahá'ís. When Bahá'ís meet, they usually greet each other by saying 'Alláh-u-Abhá'. This is the Bahá'í greeting. 'Alláh-u-Abhá' is one of the Names of God and it means 'God, the Glorious'.

When you go home (if your parents are Bahá'í), you may very politely greet them by saying Alláh-u-Abhá. Whenever you see another Bahá'í, you normally greet that person by saying Alláh-u-Abhá. This does not mean of course that you cannot greet the Bahá'ís in any other way. But generally Bahá'ís, especially when they are with other Bahá'ís only, prefer to greet each other by saying 'Alláh-u-Abhá.'"

1.5 Closing Prayer

"Can one of you please say a prayer? We should all listen silently and calmly. Saying prayers is communication with God. Prayer is like talking to God. When we say our prayers, or listen to others saying prayers, we must, of course, behave very politely and listen attentively, silently and calmly." If none of the students knows a prayer by memory, the teacher says one.

1.6 Teacher's Suggestion for the Week
"Dear children, you can go home now. Please remember that Bahá'í children, especially those, who attend these classes, must always be very polite. We will see each other again next week. Please do not forget to arrive on time for the class. Goodbye and see you all next week."

2. Cleanliness

"Alláh-u-Abhá class."

2.1 Opening Prayer
One of the students or the teacher says a prayer.

2.2 Cleanliness
"Dear children, it is very important for Bahá'í children to be clean all the time. What does it mean to be clean?" (Allow the children to respond). "To be clean means wearing tidy clothes and being physically clean by regularly washing our faces, hands, noses, ears, feet and so on.

"Dear children, you must know that it is very important to wear clean clothes and keep our bodies clean all the time. Every morning when you wash your hands and face with clean water and soap, you should also clean your ears. It is easy to do this. Wet the corner of your towel and gently clean the inner part of your ears with it. Never use a matchstick, pin or items such as these to clean your ears. It is dangerous, as you may damage your ears. Cutting your nails is also necessary. Do not let your nails grow long. If you cannot trim your nails yourself, ask your mother or an adult at home to help you. When nails become long, dirt accumulates under them. This dirt may enter your body while you are eating and makes you sick.

"Dear children, you should also, by every means possible, avoid drinking dirty water. It is very easy to get sick by drinking water, which is not clean. Please never forget this.

"Let me repeat: Bahá'í children should always be clean; wear clean clothes and have clean hands, faces, ears and bodies. You should use clean water for washing, and avoid drinking dirty water. By doing this, you will reduce the risk of getting sick and creating unnecessary trouble at home for you and your parents. Also, God wants us to be clean and healthy."

2.3 Break: Songs, Games, Student Registration and Children's Cleanliness

Song:
Teach the children the following song. (Also include other songs the children know.)

Love, Love, Love

Love, love, love, love,
Love your fellow man.
Love, love, love
Is how the world began.
God loved creation
So He created thee
To love, love, love Him
And humanity.

Love God's creatures
Be they great or small.
See each human
As a shining star.
God loved creation
So He created thee
To love, love, love Him
And humanity.

Game: "Cat and Mouse"
The children form a circle. The teacher chooses one child to be a mouse and another to be a cat. The mouse starts running. It can run in and out of the circle, across the circle, around the children or any other way it wants. The cat cannot catch the

mouse unless it goes exactly the same way. Once the cat catches the mouse, the teacher should choose another cat and another mouse, and the game continues.

2.4 Story about the Importance of Drinking Clean Water

The following is an example of such a story to tell the children about this topic.

"Dear children, I want to tell you a story. Please listen carefully so that you can repeat it to me next week."

Story:
Early one morning, mother got up and saw that her son Mulenga (the teacher should use names that are common locally) was having difficulties breathing. She put her hand on his cheeks and forehead. They were hot as if he had a fever. She woke him up and said to him, "My dear son, you appear to be sick." Mulenga, who could hardly talk, replied very gently saying, "My dear mother, I have a very bad headache."

Mulenga's mother decided to call a doctor and find out what was wrong with her son. She made a cup of light tea and gave it to Mulenga. As he had a fever, she asked him not to eat anything else until the doctor saw him. Mulenga did not feel hungry, but he drank the tea and went to sleep again. At about mid-day, the doctor came and thoroughly examined Mulenga, asking him many questions. At the end of his examination, the doctor told Mulenga's mother that her son had typhoid. He explained what kind of food and medicine Mulenga needed and advised her to follow his instructions in taking good care of her son until he had recovered.

Mulenga's mother was sad to hear that her dear boy had typhoid because she knew that it was a dangerous disease. When the doctor left, she asked Mulenga if he had drunk any dirty water in the past few days. Mulenga's mother knew that the water in their home was always clean and she always washed the vegetables very well. How could Mulenga have got typhoid?

Mulenga told his mother that a few days ago he had been playing with the other children at school. After a lot of chasing and running around, Mulenga was tired and thirsty. The children said that the tap water was warm so they drank from the nearby stream. Mulenga said, "I think that water was not clean and it has made me sick." Mother said, "Yes, my dear son, it is not good to drink dirty water. Water in the stream is not good for drinking. Germs, which cause many diseases, are often found in dirty water. I have told you many time that you must not drink dirty water. I remember you telling me how in your Bahá'í children's class your teacher also tells everyone the importance of drinking clean water. Now, you have seen how you and your parents can suffer because of drinking dirty water."

Mulenga was sick for 25 days. He had to take a lot of medicine and eat special food until he recovered. At the end, he had lost so much weight that many of his friends could not recognise him. As his illness happened during the school's examination time, Mulenga could not complete his schooling.

"Now you see my dear children how one careless act can cause a lot of problems. If Mulenga had not drunk that dirty water, he would not have been sick. You should always try to avoid things that can make you sick.

"Let us try to memorise the following quotation about cleanliness:

And although bodily cleanliness is a physical thing, it hath, nevertheless, a powerful influence on the life of the spirit.[i]

'Abdu'l-Bahá"

8

2.5 Closing Prayer
One of the students or the teacher may say a closing prayer.

2.6 Teacher's Suggestion for the Week
"Dear children please remember that Bahá'í children should be polite all the time. They greet their parents, if they are Bahá'ís, with Alláh-u-Abhá whenever they enter the house. They try to be clean when they go to their Bahá'í classes, and at all other times. Remember also that they avoid drinking dirty water. When you go home today, I want you to ask your family what they do to keep the drinking water in your house clean. This way you will know how to help keep the water clean.

"Goodbye and see you all next class."

3. Memorising a Bahá'í prayer

"Alláh-u-Abhá class."

3.1 Opening Prayer
One of the children or the teacher may say a prayer.

3.2 Review of last week's lesson on Cleanliness
"Dear children, do you remember what we discussed last time we met? Can one of you please tell us what we learned in our last class?"

The teacher may then have to ask one of the children to volunteer. Through encouragement and simple questions (see guidance given in the *Teacher's Manual for Bahá'í Children's Classes*), the teacher should try to get all, or at least most, of the children to participate in repeating what was learned last class.

3.3 Break: Songs, Games, Student Registration and Children's Cleanliness

Song:
Teach the following song to the children. (Also include other songs the children know.)

> Look at Me
>
> Look at me, follow me, be as I am
> 'Abdu'l-Bahá, 'Abdu'l-Bahá
>
> Teach the cause...
> Love mankind...
> Serve your Lord...
> Sacrifice...
> Look at me...

Game: "Relay Race"
Divide the children into two teams. Ask each team to form a line. Place two stones in the distance about 20 paces away. Give a stick to the first child in each line. When you say "go", the first child runs as fast as he can and touches the stone with the stick, then runs back to give the stick to the next person in line, who will repeat the action of the first child. The team, which finishes first, is the winner.

3.4 Memorising a Prayer

Help the children learn the following prayer in the way that was explained in Sections 2 and 3 of the *Teaching Children's Classes* manual.

> **O God, guide me, protect me, make of me a shining lamp and a brilliant star. Thou art the Mighty and the Powerful.**[ii]
>
> 'Abdu'l-Bahá

The aim is to teach the prayer so that everyone understands it word by word. Children, one by one and collectively, may be asked to say the prayer until, as a result of repetition, they understand and memorise it.

3.5 Closing Prayer

One of the students or the teacher may say the prayer.

3.6 Teacher's Suggestion for the Week

"Dear children, you memorised a Bahá'í prayer today. Please say or chant it at home every morning and every evening for the next week. This will help you memorise it better and be able to say it fluently. Goodbye and see you all next class."

4. Review of lesson # 3

"Alláh-u-Abhá class."

4.1 Opening Prayer
One of the students or the teacher may say a prayer.

4.2 Review of Last Week's Lesson
The teacher asks the students one by one, but not in a monotonous manner, to recite by heart the prayer that was memorised last week. At times, the whole class can be asked to recite the prayer together. This is done until the teacher is satisfied that everyone knows the prayer by heart. It is very important to avoid having the children become bored with this exercise, as it is easy for the young to become tired of a monotonous activity. If there are many children, the teacher may ask them to sing a song, or do some fun stretching exercises from time to time while they are learning the prayer, so that they do not lose interest.

4.3 Break: Songs, Games, Student Registration and Children's Cleanliness

Song:
Sing the songs that the children have learned.

Story: *The* Wolves and the Goats
Once there was a herd of goats that had to pass over a very old bridge to get to the pasture where the sweet grass grew. Underneath the bridge lived a family of wolves that loved to eat little goats. But the wolves were very lazy and always slept a lot, waking up only at the sound of a goat passing over the bridge. The goats were very smart and learned how to walk very lightly over the bridge without making any noise, because, of course, they did not want to wake up the wolves. They listened closely to

12   Book-1

the snoring of the wolves, and if at any moment it stopped they would stay very still, because they knew that the wolves were listening. If the goats stayed very still, the wolves would go back to sleep.

Game: "The Wolves and the Goats"
The teacher makes a bridge out of sticks and benches, some high, some low. The children must cross the bridge, going under the high sticks and over the low ones. The teacher, by clapping or hitting a pan, represents the wolves snoring. Every now and then the wolves wake up. The child has to stay still, even though he/she may have one foot up in the air, until the wolves go back to sleep. If the child knocks down a stick or even makes a small noise, the wolves wake up and gobble up the little goat.

4.4 Closing Prayer
One of the students or the teacher may say a prayer.

4.5 Teacher's Suggestion for the Week
"Dear children, for the next week, please say the prayer at home every morning and every evening. Goodbye and see you all next class."

5. Kindness to animals

"Alláh-u-Abhá class."

5.1 Opening Prayer
The teacher asks one of student to say the prayer from Lesson # 3.

5.2 Kindness to Animals
"Dear children, there are many animals that are our friends. They work for us and we benefit from them. If we did not have these animals, we would have a hard time and our lives would be difficult. Can you think of some animals that help us?" (Allow children to respond.)

After the children respond, the teacher might give a few examples, such as: "We use horses and cattle to pull carts or wagons. We can get a ride in the cart or heavy things can be carried for us. Donkeys work very hard helping us carry our heavy loads. We benefit a lot from cows, goats and sheep. We can drink their milk, we make shoes from their skins and we make clothes from their wool. Oxen plough our farms, help us weed our fields and do other agricultural work. Chickens give us eggs and meat. To summarise, we benefit from many domesticated animals. Dogs watch our homes at night. They stay outside without sleeping, even when it is very cold and wet, to protect us. Cats catch mice and, as a result, the mice do not damage our food and clothes. Bees make honey, which we enjoy eating. Some birds sing so beautifully for us.

"We should be kind to these animals. We should not trouble them, nor should we hurt them. As far as possible, we should try to make them comfortable, give them water and food and keep them warm when the weather is cold. We should not overload them. If they become sick, we should help them to become well.

We should never allow ourselves to hurt them. Remember, animals, like humans, feel pain, although they cannot talk to us or to complain about their pain. Bahá'í children should never agree to hurt an animal.

"'Abdu'l-Bahá said:

> **If an animal be sick, let the children try to heal it, if it be hungry, let them feed it, if thirsty, let them quench its thirst, if weary, let them see that it rests.**[iii]

"Bahá'í children should not even hurt animals that do not directly help us. For example: we should not hurt doves, sparrows, butterflies and other animals. They do not harm us. They all have a life to live, have a mother and a nest to go to. They do not like to be hurt.

"Of course, dear children, you must know that there are some insects that may seem to be harmful to us but are actually very useful. For instance, you may think that bees are harmful because they sting. They are very useful insects and we should avoid their sting by not harming them. But if they attack us we may have to kill a few in order to protect ourselves. There are also insects that harm our crops or our animals. We often have to control them to save our crops and animals.

"'Abdu'l-Bahá has told us to be kind to animals and never to hurt them if we can avoid it. He says:

> **Unless ye must,**
> **Bruise not the serpent in the dust...**
> **And if ye can,**
> **No ant should ye alarm...**[iv]

"This means that even a snake should only be killed if it is going to harm us. But as far as possible, we should not even hurt an ant!

Bahá'í children, therefore, should be careful not to step on ants when they walk, because ants also have a life to live and their life is dear and sweet to them.

"Dear children please memorise this quote from 'Abdu'l-Bahá'. I will say it to you and you can repeat it after me, one word at a time, until you have learned it."

The teacher repeats the first few words a few times and asks the children to recite it together as a group. This is done bit by bit until the children have memorised the quotation.

"Dear children, I would like you to memorise this quotation for next week. Next week I am going to tell you a story about how a child was very kind to an animal."

5.3 Break: Songs, Games, Student Registration and Children's Cleanliness

Song:
Teach the following song to the children. Also include other songs they know.

God's Creatures

The creatures of this big world,
Whether they walk or fly, or fly,
Are part of God's creation
Like you and I

Chorus:
That's why we treat them with kindness.
Remember when you do, you do.
To care for God's creation
Brings blessing to you.

The dog on our front door step,

He is our faithful friend, our friend.
We also thank our milk cow
And bees in the wind.
(Chorus)

The donkey carries his burden,
The kitty purrs on our lap, our lap,
And the birds sing sweetly
When we take our nap.
(Chorus)

Game: "Duck, Duck, Chicken"
Ask the class to sit in a circle. Choose one child to be the "duck". The duck walks around the outside of the circle touching the other children's head saying "duck, duck, duck...." Then he/she touches one of the children's head and say "chicken". The child who is touched becomes the chicken. The chicken gets up and chases the duck around the circle, trying to catch the duck. The duck runs to the empty space left by the chicken. If the duck is caught before reaching the empty space, the duck goes to the middle of the circle. If the chicken does not catch the duck, the chicken continues walking around the circle touching the children's heads saying "duck, duck, duck...", and the game continues.

5.4 Learning Some Words of 'Abdu'l-Bahá
The teacher asks the children to repeat the sentence they learned about kindness to animals.

5.5 Closing Prayer
One of the children says the prayer of Lesson # 3.

5.6 Teacher's Suggestion for the Week
"Dear children, please memorise the quote from 'Abdu'l-Bahá. Remember, do your best never to hurt any animal. Goodbye and see you all next class."

6. Kindness to animals

"Alláh-u-Abhá class."

6.1 Opening Prayer
One of the students says the prayer from Lesson # 3.

6.2 Review Last Week's Lesson
The teacher asks some questions about the previous lesson. A few of the children can also be asked to recite the quotation by heart. Care must be taken that this question and answer period does not become too long and boring for the children.

6.3 Break: Songs, Games, Student Registration and Children's Cleanliness

Song:
Review the song from last lesson (God's Creatures), and sing other songs the children know.

Game: "Poor Kitty"
Ask the children to form a circle and sit down. Choose a child to be the "kitty" (a small cat). The kitty goes to the middle of the circle. The kitty must try to walk like a cat. The child goes up to one of the other children and says, "meow" several times trying to make the child laugh. The child should pet the kitty and say "poor kitty" three times without smiling or laughing. If the child does not laugh or smile, then kitty goes to another child and "meows". But if the child laughs or smiles, then he/she becomes the kitty, and the game continues.

6.4 Story Telling
The teacher may change the story to suit local conditions and children's understanding. Some suggestions have been made in the text.

"Dear children, last week I promised to tell you a story. Please be attentive and listen carefully so you understand it well. I want you to share it with your parents, brothers, sisters and other relatives who live with you at home."

Story:
One day, when the weather was cold and wet a seven-year- old boy was coming home from school. He was alone. None of his classmates were with him since he had to stay behind at school to finish his work. He had his school bag on his shoulder and, because of the cold weather, he had his hands deep in his pockets. It was very cold and very wet.

The boy was walking quickly with his head down. He wanted to reach home soon and get warm. As he was walking, and thinking to himself that when he gets home, his mother would have a warm room and delicious food ready for him. He imagined that, as he arrived home, he would take off his heavy wet clothes, and would sit next to the fire drinking hot tea, after which his mother would bring him a bowl of hot soup.

As he was quickly walking along, deep in thought, he heard the groaning of an animal, which sounded like the loud cry of a little baby who had lost its mother. At first, the boy wanted to ignore it and pass by. But when he heard the cry again, he stopped. When he listened carefully, he realised that the noise sounded like a little kitten, although it could not be seen. As he looked around carefully, he saw a beautiful little white kitten lying in the cold mud meowing (crying).

(The teacher may ask the children if they know the sound of a kitten meowing.)

As the boy got closer, he saw that the animal was shivering, because of the cold. He felt sorry for the kitten and immediately picked it up. He realised that the animal was cold and wet. It had a runny nose and eyes. He held the kitten gently in his arms to take it home.

As soon as the animal felt a little bit of warmth in the boy's arms, its legs started to move. It looked with great love and appreciation at the boy, as if it was thanking him in its own language, saying: "Thank you good boy. You are very kind. If you had not found me I would certainly have died at night because of the cold. What a very good boy you are. More than one hundred people have passed me since morning and have heard my cry. But none of them was kind to me. It just shows that you are a very good and a very kind boy. Thank you. I am grateful to you. I will promise to help and serve you. I will compensate you for your kindness."

The boy could read all these kind words in the kitten's loving eyes. He kept stroking it on the way home. When he arrived, his mother saw him putting down a nice white kitten from under his warm coat. She asked him where he got the kitten? He explained to his mother what had happened. The mother was proud of her son because of his kind action. She said, "Well done! My good boy! How kind and nice you are you for showing kindness to animals. God is also pleased with this action of yours." She prepared a place for the kitten in a corner of the room. She gave the kitten some milk and made sure that the animal was comfortable.

The kitten grew up in their home. It protected their home from mice and, whenever it saw the boy or other members of the household, it would go and rub its head and body against them, trying to thank them in it's own special way for their kindness.

The teacher can ask the children if they liked the story, and ask questions about it to see if they can remember the details.

"Dear children, I would like you to tell me this story next week."

6.5 Closing Prayer
One of the children says the prayer from Lesson # 3.

6.6 Teacher's Suggestions for the Week
"Dear children remember to always be kind to animals. 'Abdu'l-Bahá says: **"And if ye can, no ant should ye alarm."** Also remember to tell the story I told you today to your parents, brothers, sisters and anyone else who lives at home with you. Goodbye and see you all next class."

7. Obedience to parents

"Alláh-u-Abhá class."

7.1 Opening Prayer
One of the students says the prayer from Lesson # 3.

7.2 Review of Last Week's Lesson
The teacher should lead a discussion in which a few of the students will take part by repeating last week's story. This is a very useful exercise for helping the children become fluent in language and to strengthen their power of speech. However, care must be taken not to let them get bored, as children at this tender age can easily become tired of a monotonous exercise. The teacher must be alert and change the subject if and when necessary.

7.3 Break: Songs, Games, Student Registration and Children's Cleanliness

Song:
Teach the following song to the children, and also sing other songs they know.

<u>Prefer Your Brother</u>

Chorus:
It is a blessing to prefer your brother,
This is a way to show you care.
It is a blessing to prefer your sister,
You are richer, the more you share.

I am thirsty, I am thirsty,
But my brother, he comes first.
So I offer him the water
That will quench his thirst.

(Chorus)

I am hungry, I am hungry,
And my sister, she is too.
So I give her some of my food,
That's what's best to do.
(Chorus)

Game: "Square, Circle, Triangle"
The teacher names a sequence of three shapes (for instance: circle, circle, square) and asks one of the children to repeat it. Then the child is asked to try to draw the sequence. If the child cannot remember a sequence of three, use a sequence of two. If a sequence of three is too easy, use four.

Variations:

a. Instead of giving the sequence verbally, prepare some cards with different sequences drawn on them. Show one of the cards to each child and after having looked at it, he/she repeats the sequence, first aloud and then by drawing it on paper.

b. This can be done with sequences of actions. For example: jump, turn, touch your toes, touch your nose, clap, take a step forward, etc.

7.4 Obedience to Parents
The following is an example of how the teacher can discuss obedience to parents with the children:

"Dear children, you all know very well that parents do a lot for their children. Day and night they think of them. They do many things for their sake and sometimes they sacrifice their own comfort for them. From the day a child is born, the mother begins working hard to take care of the baby. During the day she works hard, and at night she hardly sleeps. According to how much money they have both parents try hard to make their children comfortable. Parents, one may say, truly sacrifice their lives for their children.

"In return, children must love their parents and show them respect. They should always try not to displease them and never say or do things that will bring grief and sadness to their hearts. Children should always obey their parents.

"Dear children, let us think about something. If you work hard to make a doll or a wire bicycle or any other toy, you love it very much. You would never agree to let someone else destroy it. Or, for example, if you were to sow a seed of a plant, water it, protect it and take care of it, until it grows into a big plant, you would never allow someone else to destroy it. In the same way, your parents, who love you very much, work very hard for your sake. In addition, God has bestowed love of the children in the hearts of the parents. They love you as they love themselves, even more! In return, you must also love them and obey them.

"All the Messengers of God have told us that children must respect their parents. Bahá'u'lláh says that obedience to one's parents is like obedience to God. So, my dear children, you should listen to this counsel from God and His Messengers and never do anything that will bring grief and displeasure to your parents. You must always obey them, respect them and love them."

Story:
A very poor mother had a small baby boy. One night, when the weather was very cold and raining hard, she was sitting in her small house with its windows covered with paper instead of glass. She was shivering from cold and had no firewood to heat the room. As the mother looked at her baby, she was afraid that her innocent child might die of the cold during the night, and her heart beat faster. She tried to think what to do but she could not

think of anything. Her tears started to roll down her cold face. Finally, she took off her clothes, wrapped her baby in them, and held him tight in her arms for the whole night. In the morning, when the neighbours came to see the poor woman, she was very sick with a terrible cold, but the baby was warm in her arms. She recovered after a few days, and continued with her life and enjoyed her baby.

"There are many stories like this where the mother has sacrificed her life for her children. Dear children, you must value your parents and never displease them."

7.5 Closing Prayer
One of the students says the prayer of Lesson # 3.

7.6 Teacher's Suggestion for the Week
"Dear children, always obey your parents, respect them and love them. Goodbye and see you all next class."

8. Cleanliness

"Alláh-u-Abhá class."

8.1 Opening Prayer
One of the children says the prayer from Lesson # 3.

8.2 Review Last Week's Lesson
The teacher begins by asking questions about last week's lesson on obedience to our parents to see what the children can remember. The teacher can also ask questions about the story.

8.3 Break: Songs, Games, Student Registration and Children's Cleanliness

Song:
Teach the following song to the children, and sing others songs they know.

<u>God Is One</u>

God is one, man is one
And all the religions are one.
Land and sea, hill and valley,
Under the beautiful sun.

Chorus:
God is one, man is one,
And all the religions agree,
When everyone learns   }
The three onenesses   } (x2)
We'll have world unity. }

God is love, God is light
And all are as one in His sight.
Black and white, brown and yellow,

This is the time to unite.
(Chorus)

Game: "The Hidden Quality"
All the children form a circle with their hands held out in front of them. The teacher holds a coin or stone in his/her hand. The coin represents a quality, for example, "kindness". Then as the teacher walks along, and passes his/her hands over the hands of each child and says, "John is kind, Musonda is kind, etc." Each child closes his/her hands, acting as though the teacher has given him/her the coin. The teacher actually leaves the coin in the hands of one of the children. When the teacher has gone around the entire circle, one child tries to guess who has the coin by saying; for example, "Jane is very kind". Then Jane should open her hands and show whether she has the coin or not. The child has three guesses to try to find out who has the coin, after which the game is repeated using another quality.

8.4 The Necessity of Observing Cleanliness (Being Clean)

The following is an example of how this topic may be discussed with the children:

"Dear children, do you recall when we talked about cleanliness?

'Abdu'l-Bahá said:

> **And although bodily cleanliness is a physical thing, it hath, nevertheless, a powerful influence on the life of the spirit.**[v]

(The teacher will need to help the children understand this quote.)

"A Bahá'í is a person who believes and obeys Bahá'u'lláh. It would be meaningless for anyone to call himself/herself a Bahá'í and not try to follow the teachings of Bahá'u'lláh. We are all

Bahá'ís. We should, therefore, try our best to live the way Bahá'u'lláh teaches us to.

"Baha'u'lláh has told us to keep ourselves clean and to be the very essence of cleanliness amongst mankind. This means that we should try hard to keep our bodies clean and neat all the time and to wear clean clothes. When we do so, people are going to notice that Bahá'ís, following the teachings of Bahá'u'lláh, are always clean and neat. So, as Bahá'ís, adults and children alike, should always try to be clean and orderly if we want to obey Bahá'u'lláh.

"In today's lesson, I am going to tell you three important things about being clean. Please listen carefully and remember them so that you can follow them and, by doing so, make Bahá'u'lláh happy with you.

1. First, trim (cut) your nails regularly and do not let them grow long. As soon as you see your nails are getting long, trim them. If you cannot do it yourself, ask your parents or an adult to help you. This is one of Bahá'u'lláh's instructions to us, to keep our nails trimmed. Dear children, I hope you understand what I am saying to you? If so, you will never let your nails grow long; either you will trim them or ask an adult to help you do so.

2. Wash your bodies with clean water regularly. Where there is no water for daily washing, wash as often as possible. If you cannot wash yourself, ask your mother or father to wash you. This is another instruction from Bahá'u'lláh to us. God willing, when you grow up, you will better understand how important these laws of Bahá'u'lláh are for us. Following this law is very important for your health.

3. When eating, it is important that your hands and the utensils you use are all clean. You should always wash your hands, with clean water, before eating. It is not a good idea for many people to use the same water to wash their hands, because this makes the water dirty." (The teacher may demonstrate how water soon

becomes dirty after one person washes his/her hands in a bowl.) "It is better to pour a small amount of clean water over your hands when you wash your hands." (The teacher can show the children how to do this by pouring a small amount of clean water over the children's hands as they wash.) "It is also good for each person who is eating to have his/her own plate.

"Today, we have learned three things about being clean. Do you remember what these things were?" (The teacher should ask the children to respond). "First, was the trimming of nails; second, regularly washing our bodies; and third was observing cleanliness when eating. I am sure that you, dear children, will follow these teachings of Bahá'u'lláh. Remember, Bahá'u'lláh is happy with whoever obeys Him."

8.5 Closing Prayer
One of the children may say the prayer from Lesson # 3.

8.6 Teacher's Suggestion for the Week
"Dear children, try to always keep yourselves clean and immaculate. Goodbye and see you all next class."

9. Cleanliness

"Alláh-u-Abhá class."

9.1 Opening Prayer
One of the students says the prayer from Lesson # 3.

9.2 Review Last Week's Lesson
The teacher begins a discussion that would lead into a review of
the previous week's lesson. "Dear children, in the last lesson, I told
you three things about being clean and neat. Do you remember
what they are?" (Allow children to respond.) "You should know
them and act upon them."

9.3 Break: Songs, Games, Student Registration and Children's Cleanliness

Song:
Teach the following song to the children, and also sing other
songs they know.

> Tell the Truth
> Chorus:
> When you tell the truth,
> (When you tell the truth)
> You win people's trust,
> (You win people's trust,)
> Always tell the truth,
> You must, you must.
>
> When you tell the truth,
> You'll never feel ashamed
> God will be pleased with you.
> If you tell a lie,
> You surely will be blamed,

And maybe lose a friend or two!
(Chorus)

Game: "Copy the Picture"
Before class, the teacher draws pictures, on paper or cards, of
stick people in different positions. Ten to fifteen pictures are
sufficient for this game. In class, the children should stand up
and spread out so that each one has enough space to freely wave
their arms about. Then the teacher tells them that they will hold
up pictures of people making different shapes with their bodies,
and the class must try to form the same shape with their own
body.

Variation:
The teacher might draw pictures of two stick people doing things
together. The children would then work in pairs.

9.4 The Necessity of Observing Cleanliness (Being Clean)

The following is an example of how this topic may be discussed
with the children:

"Today children, I want to tell you some more important points
about being clean. Please listen carefully and try to follow them as
well.

1. Wash your feet regularly. Wash your feet at least once a day
   when the weather is warm (summer) and at least once every
   three days during the cold months (winter). This is another
   instruction that Bahá'u'lláh has given to us. Remember, Bahá'ís
   should never neglect what Bahá'u'lláh has told us to do. So,
   remember: wash your feet regularly.

2. Brush your teeth regularly. Do so after every meal or at least once in the morning and once in the evening after eating and before you go to bed. Use a toothbrush and toothpaste if you have them. Otherwise use other means available to you. (The teacher can talk about other things to use for brushing teeth.)

3. Ask your mother or father to try to have a separate towel at home for each person. Towels do not have to be the expensive type. They can be made of inexpensive cloth materials at home. Whether we use towels bought from a store or we make them at home. It is important for each person at home to have their own towel and not to use other people's towels. Talk to your parents to help you with this matter.

"Dear children, I am sure you remember all the points we have discussed about cleanliness and you will try to practice them. I am going to repeat all of them for you once again in order to help you remember them well:

1. Trim your nails and do not let them become long.
2. Bathe or wash regularly.
3. Observe cleanliness when eating.
4. If bathing regularly is not possible, wash your feet regularly.
5. Brush your teeth after every meal or at least twice a day, in the morning and in the evening
6. Keep a separate towel and use your own towel."

9.5 Closing Prayer
One of the students says the prayer from Lesson # 3.

9.6 Teacher's Suggestion for the Week
"I am sure you will do your best to practice all the things we have discussed about cleanliness. Goodbye and see you all next class."

10. Being a Bahá'í

"Alláh-u-Abhá class."

10.1 Opening Prayer
One of the students says the prayer from Lesson # 3.

10.2 Review Last Week's Lesson
The teacher asks the children to recall the six points about cleanliness that they learned during the last class.

10.3 Break: Songs, Games, Student Registration and Children's Cleanliness

Song:
Teach the following song to the children, and also sing other songs they know.

I Have Found Bahá'u'lláh

I have found Bahá'u'lláh
In the early days of my life.
I will stay with him
Now and forever,
Now and forever.

Alláh-u-Abhá, Alláh-u-Abhá
Alláh-u-Abhá, now and forever.

Game: "Guessing Game"
1. Ask the children to sit in a circle.
2. Blindfold one child. Make him/her walk around the children.
3. Ask the child to touch the face and hair of one of the children in the circle. The blindfolded child must guess whom he/she is touching. If the child can guess the name of the person

correctly, he/she can sit. Then it is the turn of the child, whose name was guessed, to be blindfolded.

10.4 Being a Bahá'í

The following is one way of conversing with the children when presenting this subject.

"Dear children, you know that we are Bahá'ís. As Bahá'ís, we believe in Bahá'u'lláh. If our parents are Bahá'ís, we should be thankful to God who has been kind and gracious in guiding our parents to the right path to accept His Messenger for today, Bahá'u'lláh. We must be thankful to God for having been born in a Bahá'í family and for being raised by our parents as Bahá'í children.

"To help you appreciate what we have as Bahá'ís, I am going to tell you a story. Please listen carefully to see if you understand the message.

Story:

In a town there is a school that has many teachers and many classes, ranging from grade one to grade twelve. All the teachers are kind, knowledgeable and capable of teaching those who go to their class. There is even a university for students who want to go and learn more. Some students leave the school after finishing grade one, some after grade two, and some after finishing grade seven. There are some that will enter secondary school but leave after grade nine. Some students love all the teachers and enjoy learning more and more. The students know that they will have different teachers as they advance. Some will finish secondary school, and some will go to university and increase their understanding and knowledge even more.

Those who leave school early do not understand the knowledge taught in the higher grades in university. The earlier they leave the school, the less they know about some of the scientific subjects. Yet all the knowledge exists. The difference between the people is that some leave school earlier, some later, and some continue to learn and believe that learning never ends.

"By becoming a Bahá'í, we begin to learn about God. We believe in all of God's Messengers and Their Books. God has helped us to enter the University of the Knowledge of God which, has been brought to us by Bahá'u'lláh. Bahá'u'lláh is the Messenger of God for today. Bahá'u'lláh says that we must accept all the Religions of God and love all His people, whatever their religion and background. We believe in Bahá'u'lláh and can see the beauty of His Revelation. We recognise His teachings and try to follow them.

"We should thank Bahá'u'lláh day and night for the precious gift of His message. We should also thank our parents for allowing us to come to these classes to learn about the precious gift of the Message of Bahá'u'lláh. To show our gratitude to God, we should live according to the teachings of Bahá'u'lláh."

10.5 Closing Prayer
One of the students says the prayer from Lesson # 3.

10.6 Teacher's Suggestion for the Week
"Dear children, we should be thankful for the efforts of our parents in becoming Bahá'í. We should also appreciate the bounty of being born in a Bahá'í family. We should always strive to follow the teachings of Bahá'u'lláh. Goodbye and see you all next class."

11. Memorising a second Bahá'í prayer

"Alláh-u-Abhá class."

11.1 Opening Prayer
One of the children says the prayer from Lesson # 3.

11.2 Review Last Week's Lesson
Teacher reviews the previous lesson by asking the students questions.

11.3 Break: Songs, Games, Student Registration and Children's Cleanliness

Song:
Teach the following song to the children, and also sing other songs they know.

Come and Join Us.

We are flowers in God's garden,
We are leaves of one tree

Chorus:
Come and join us,
In our quest for unity,
It's the way of life for you and me.

All the earth is one country,
Man is one, can't you see?
(Chorus)

Black and white, red and yellow,
Man is one, can't you see?

(Chorus)

God is one, men are brothers,
And religions all agree.
(Chorus)

Lunda and Lozi, Bemba and Tonga,
All are brothers to you and me,
(Chorus)

Game: "Giants"
Two children stand side by side and the left leg of one child is tied to the right leg of the other child. Then they walk from one place to another.

Variations:
a. Three, four or more children are tied to one another and they all attempt to walk together.
b. Obstacles can be placed along the path, such as branches and stones, making sure it is done in a safe way.
c. Instead of walking, the children jump like frogs, walk like crabs, etc.

11.4 Learning a Prayer

Help the children learn the following prayer in the way that was explained in Sections 2 and 3 of the "Teaching Children's Classes" manual.

> **He is God! O <u>Divine providence</u>, <u>shed</u> a <u>ray</u> from the Sun of Truth upon this gathering that it may become illumined.**[vi]
>
> *'Abdu'l-Bahá*

The words, which are underlined, might be explained to the children using the following examples.

Divine - heavenly or celestial

providence - someone who cares for or guides

shed - give or pour

Sun of Truth - refers to the Prophets of God, Bahá'u'lláh for this dispensation.

illumined - made light. Example: The room was dark at night. When mother lit a candle, it **illumined** the room and she could see everyone's faces.

The aim is to teach the prayer so that everyone understands it word by word. Children, one by one and collectively, may be asked to say the prayer until, as a result of repetition, they understand and memorise it.

11.5 Closing Prayer
One of the students says the prayer from Lesson # 3.

11.6 Teacher's Suggestion for the Week
"Dear children, please say the prayer we learned today at home every morning and every evening. Goodbye and see you all next class."

12. 'Abdu'l-Bahá

"Alláh-u-Abhá class."

12.1 Opening Prayer
One of the children says the prayer from Lesson # 3.

12.2 Review Last Week's Lesson
The teacher asks the children to say the prayer they learned the previous week.   If the number of children in the class is not too large, each child may be given the opportunity to say the prayer.

12.3 Break: Songs, Games, Student Registration and Children's Cleanliness

Song:
Teach the following song to the children, and also sing other songs they know. The teacher should explain who "the Master" (Abdu'l-Bahá) is, and that today they will be learning about Him.

That Is How Bahá'í s Should Be

I love the Master,
The Master loves me.
He shows me how Bahá'ís should be.
Trusting in God faithfully,
That is how Bahá'ís should be.

I love the Master,
The Master loves me.
He shows me how Bahá'ís should be.
Praying for guidance constantly,
That is how Bahá'ís should be.
I love the Master,
The Master loves me.

He shows me how Bahá'ís should be.
God's will, not my will my prayer will be,
That is how Bahá'ís should be.

Game: " Touch Telephone"
Several children stand in a line, one behind the other, all looking towards the front. The person at the front of the line is looking at a piece of paper hanging on a wall or tree or, if available, at a blackboard. More than one line can be organised if necessary. With a finger, the teacher draws something on the back of the last child. The child, in turn, draws on the back of the child in front of him/her, and so on, until the child at the front is reached. After the picture is drawn on his/her back, he/she then draws it on the piece of paper or blackboard. The teacher draws next to it what he/she had drawn on the back of the first child, to see if it is the same or whether it has changed along the way. The drawings should be simple so that all the children can do them. (Note: If no paper is available, the child can simply draw the picture with a stick on the ground.)

12.4 'Abdu'l-Bahá
Have a selection of photographs of 'Abdu'l-Bahá and show one of them to the children. The lesson may be presented as follows:

"Dear children, you may have seen this photograph in your house. Your mother or father may have told you that this is the photograph of 'Abdu'l-Bahá. 'Abdu'l-Bahá loved children very much. He always hugged the children and had great love and affection for them.

'Abdu'l-Bahá said:
> **Children are the ornaments of the home. A home without children is like a home light.**[vii]

He said that children are the ornaments of every house and a house without children is like a room with no light. Do you know what an ornament is? (Ornament - something that decorates and makes a place beautiful.)

"Abdu'l-Bahá said that parents should never beat their children nor subject them to abusive language. 'Abdu'l-Bahá was like a father to the orphans, a help to the widows and a refuge to the poor. He had great compassion for the destitute. 'Abdu'l-Bahá always told us not to harm animals.

"Abdu'l-Bahá has taught us many things. After Bahá'u'lláh, He was our Guide and Teacher. 'Abdu'l-Bahá always sacrificed His comfort for our peace and happiness. There are many stories like this about 'Abdu'l-Bahá. Often a big crowd of men, women and children would stand in the narrow alleys of 'Akka, the city where 'Abdu'l-Bahá lived. Everyone in the crowd wore torn clothes, looked pale, miserable and was very thin and weak. Women would be standing holding their thin babies, while the older children aged 5 or 6 years, would stand in a row. 'Abdu'l-Bahá would arrive and give a little bit of money to everyone. He would ask about everyone's health and well being. Every weekend, 'Abdu'l-Bahá would do similar things to help the poor. When the weather was cold, He would give clothes to the poor, and sometimes would even help them put the clothes on."

Story:
One of 'Abdu'l-Bahá's gardeners had a dog. One day, the gardener decided to punish the dog by keeping it in a room for the whole night without any food, because of something the dog had done. The next day, at dawn, when the gardener was still asleep, 'Abdu'l-Bahá came to his house. The gardener woke up suddenly and bowed down respectfully in front of 'Abdu'l-Bahá. 'Abdu'l-Bahá asked him why he had punished the dog and had not given it food. "Don't you know that it is a sin to hurt the animals and we should never harm them? Hurry up and free the animal." The gardener immediately opened the door of the room where the dog was imprisoned and freed it. The dog came out and lay at

'Abdu'l-Bahá's feet. 'Abdu'l-Bahá asked the gardener what he had in the house to give to the dog. The gardener said he had nothing except a few sugar cubes. 'Abdu'l-Bahá asked for some and gave them to the dog. The dog was so hungry that it swallowed the sugar cubes and rubbed itself on 'Abdu'l-Bahá's feet. 'Abdu'l-Bahá told the gardener to prepare some food for the poor dog and to never punish it in that way again.

Note:
The teacher should have a good selection of photographs of 'Abdu'l-Bahá, especially those where He is showing love and affection for children. The teacher should also do his/her utmost to help the children know more about 'Abdu'l-Bahá, to develop a deep love for Him and to obey His wishes. This can be done by telling stories about Him to the children whenever possible.

12.5 Closing Prayer
One of the children says a prayer to close the lesson.

12.6 Teacher's Suggestion for the Week
"Dear children, please tell your mothers and your family what you learned today about 'Abdu'l-Bahá. Goodbye and see you all next class."

13. Cleanliness

"Alláh-u-Abhá class."

13.1 Opening Prayer
One of the students says the prayer from Lesson # 11.

13.2 Review Last Week's Lesson
The teacher talks about 'Abdu'l-Bahá and asks questions about Him from the previous lesson.

13.3 Break: Songs, Games, Student Registration and Children's Cleanliness

Song:
Teach the following song to the children, and also sing other songs they know.

<u>My Love Is My Stronghold</u>

> O Son of Being!
> My love is My stronghold,
> He that entereth therein
> Is safe and secure,
> He that turneth away
> Shall surely stray and perish.
>
> O Son of Being!
> My love is My stronghold.
> O Son of Being!
> My love is My stronghold.

Game: "The Blind Man"
One child is blindfolded. Another child acts as a guide and leads blindfolded child around. The "guide" will need to be reminded

that his blindfolded partner trusts that person and he/she must be careful, nothing happens to the blindfolded child.

Variations:
a. Rows of blindfolded children form a train and someone guides them.
b. The blindfolded child is guided around obstacles (tree trunks, ditches, rocks, tires, etc.).
c. To increase the children's capacity for giving and receiving instructions, the blindfolded child can be guided just by someone's voice. The guide (and perhaps the teacher) follows close by to catch the child in case he/she stumbles.

13.4 The Necessity of Observing Cleanliness

The teacher may begin a conversation with the children, such as the following, on the subject:

"Dear children, remember we have so far talked a few times about cleanliness. I told you that Bahá'u'lláh and 'Abdu'l-Bahá have both encouraged us strongly to be clean all the time. This means that our bodies and clothes must be, as far as possible, so clean that people will realise that Bahá'ís follow the teachings of Bahá'u'lláh and try to be clean all the time. You remember we learned that Bahá'í children, in order to be clean, should (the teacher can ask the children to recall these):

- Trim their nails regularly
- Bathe regularly
- Observe cleanliness when eating
- Wash their feet regularly, if regular washing of the whole body is not possible
- Brush their teeth regularly, at least twice a day
- Have and use their own towel

"Today, I want to continue to talk about cleanliness because this is a very important subject. We will discuss it further until you master its importance. As Bahá'í children, try to be clean and neat all the time. Today we will talk about three more things related to being clean.

"Dear children:
1. Never forget to comb your hair. It is very important to comb our hair every morning when we wake up. Bahá'u'lláh says God has given us hair as an adornment to our heads. Hair makes us more beautiful and attractive. We should, therefore, take care of it, keep it clean and tidy, and comb it always.

2. Make sure that you wear clean clothes. When clothes are dirty they should be washed.

3. If you have shoes, clean and dust them regularly. Dust them with a simple piece of cloth that is kept for this purpose, or with a special shoe brush. Try always, to keep your shoes polished and clean. This makes a difference in how clean one looks. Some shoes cannot be polished but all shoes can be kept clean.

"Let me repeat what I have told you today about cleanliness so that you may remember it well:
- Comb you hair regularly
- Wear clean clothes
- Keep your shoes clean and shiny

"I hope you will remember what we discussed about cleanliness today and during the previous lessons. I also hope that you will try to practice them so that you will always be clean and neat. By doing so, Bahá'u'lláh will be very happy with you."

13.5 Closing Prayer
One of the students says the prayer from Lesson # 11.

13.6 Teacher's Suggestion for the Week
"Dear children, always be clean and neat. Goodbye and see you all next class."

14. "Trees in the garden" play

"Alláh-u-Abhá class."

14.1 Opening Prayer
One of the students says the prayer from Lesson # 11.

14.2 Review Last Week's Lesson
The teacher asks children questions and helps them review the three points about cleanliness from the previous lesson.

14.3 Break: Songs, Games, Student Registration and Children's Cleanliness

Song:
Sing a few songs that the children already know.

Game: "The Twins"
Divide the children into pairs. They should be about the same size. The two children sit back to back. Then they hook elbows and try to stand up. This can also be tried with groups of three or four, after the children have practised a bit.

14.4 Learning the "Trees in the Garden" Play
The teacher can ask the children if they know what a play is, and then explain that today they are going to learn a play. The teacher can then begin by telling the children the story of the play, so they know what it is about. The teacher should describe how the scene will look, and how the children will be standing

Below is a description of the scene. The play follows after it.

The scene:
A number of students stand next to each other forming a square, like the four walls of a garden. Two of the students form the gate of

the garden. When the two are standing close to each other, the gate is closed. To open it, one turns to the right and the other to the left. Children should stand in such a way that the audience is able to see inside the garden.

Inside the garden, one student is a mango tree, another is a guava tree and the third is a banana tree. The fruits of each tree are made of paper and are pinned on each child's chest. A few children are also standing as fruitless trees (no fruits on their chests) in one of the corners of the garden. Before the play starts, the gate of the garden is closed.

The play begins with the gate opening. A gardener and his visitor enter the garden.

Visitor: *(After looking around, turns to the gardener and speaks)* What a wonderful and beautiful garden. There are so many trees full of fruit. You must have worked very hard. I would like to know what you did to cause the trees to have so much fruit.

Gardener: My trees can all speak. Ask them your question.

Visitor: *(getting close to the mango tree)* What kind of fruit tree are you?

Mango tree: I am a mango tree. When I was very small, the gardener planted me in this garden. He gave me water and looked after me. My roots gave me food and my leaves gave me air until I grew up into a big tree. The gardener loves me very much. Day and night, he takes care of me. Now I give fruit for the gardener to sell. People love my fruit and enjoy eating it.

Visitor: Thank you for telling me the story of your life. *(The visitor gets close to the guava tree)* Tell me what kind of tree are you and how did you come to this garden?

Guava tree: I am a guava tree. The gardener got me as a small tree and planted me here. With great care, he gave me water and looked after me. He cut my dead branches and I grew day by day. Now that I have grown up, everyone enjoys my fruit and the gardener can sell it.

Visitor: I am so happy to see such wonderful trees in this garden. (*Moving towards the banana*) What kind of tree are you?

Banana tree: I am a banana tree. My story is similar to that of my other two friends. People also like my fruit, enjoy it and benefit from it in different ways.

Visitor: I am so happy with all of you. I am so happy with the gardener who has worked so hard to bring you all up.

Gardener: (*As the visitor gets close to the fruitless trees*) Those are fruitless trees. They do not give fruit. They are not useful to me. No matter what I do, they do not give fruit. (*The fruitless trees bend their heads down in sadness*).

Visitor: Shouldn't we cut them down?

Gardener: (*Shouting*) Boys, bring some axes!
(*A few boys with paper axes arrive in the garden. The gardener asks them to cut the fruitless trees. The trees start to cry. The gate of the garden closes*).

Gardener: (*turning to the audience*) We can learn a lesson from the fruit trees. When we do good things and help others we are like the trees that give good fruit.

END OF PLAY

Note:

The teacher may divide the roles for the play amongst the children. Children would have to be assisted to learn and perform their role. With practice they will all learn how to do it.

14.5 Closing Prayer

One of the students says the prayer from Lesson # 11.

14.6 Teacher's Suggestion for the Week

"Dear children, please try to remember the 'Trees in the Garden' play. We will practice it again and again, so that we can perform it later on. Goodbye and see you all next class."

15. "Trees in the Garden" play - continued

"Alláh-u-Abhá class."

15.1 Opening Prayer
One of the students says the prayer from Lesson # 11

15.2 Break: Songs, Games, Student Registration and Children's Cleanliness

Song:
Teach the following song to the children, and also sing other songs they know.

<u>If You're Happy and You Know It</u>

If you're happy and you know it
Clap your hands   (clap, clap)

If you're happy and you know it
Clap your hands   (clap, clap)

If you're happy and you know it
And you really want to show it   If
you're happy and you know it   Clap
your hands   (clap, clap)

Repeat with these actions:
- stomp your feet
- shout "hooray!"
- do all three! (clap, clap, stomp, stomp, "hooray!")

Game: "The Bridge"
A line is established on the floor using benches (or boards or even string) and it is called "the bridge". Two groups of children have to cross the bridge at the same time, going in opposite directions, without letting any one fall off the bridge. The children have to help each other change places, passing each other one by one.

15.3 Learning the "Trees in the Garden" Play
The teacher asks the students to practice the "Trees in the Garden" play, which they learned the previous class.

15.4 Closing Prayer
One of the students says prayer from Lesson # 11.

15.5 Teacher's Suggestion for the Week
"Dear children, learn this play well. You can practice it at home if you like. Goodbye and see you all next class."

16. Being a student of Bahá'í children's classes

"Alláh-u-Abhá class."

16.1 Opening Prayer
One of the students says the prayer from Lesson # 11.

16.2 Repetition of the "Trees in the Garden" Play
The teacher asks the students to repeat the "Trees in the Garden" play.

16.3 Break: Songs, Games, Student Registration and Children's Cleanliness

Songs:
Sing a few songs that the children already know.

Game: "The Snail"
All the children line up holding hands. The children at one end of the line stand in place, while the others begin to walk around them. Little by little they will wind themselves into a spiral, to form a snail.

Variations:
a. Those at one end begin to turn in a circle, winding the others up around them.
   Be careful they do not step on each other's feet.
b. Once the snail is formed, those in the middle can squat down and go under the legs of the others -- with none of the children letting go of each other's hands.

16.4 Being a Student of Bahá'í Children's Classes

"Dear children, if someone asks you what it means to be a student of the Bahá'í Children's Classes, here is how you should respond:

'I am a student of the Bahá'í Children's Classes. Every morning, I get up early, wash my face and hands with clean water and soap, brush my teeth, dry my face using my own towel, comb my hair and then I start to say my prayers. So far I have memorised two prayers. I put on my clean clothes and shoes and saying "Alláh-u-Abhá" to my parents (for the children of non-Bahá'í parents, say, "I greet my parents with love and respect"), On the weekends, I start off for my Bahá'í Children's Class. While walking along the streets, I am very polite. When I enter my Bahá'í class, I greet my teacher with "Alláh-u-Abhá." I have learnt, as a Bahá'í, to bathe regularly, I trim my nails, I wash my hands before I eat, and, when taking a regular bath is not possible, I wash my feet regularly. I am kind to animals and try to be clean and neat all the time. I show respect to my parents and I obey their instructions. I do all these things because I obey the teachings of Bahá'u'lláh.'

"This is how a student of Bahá'í Children's Classes, year one, can be described. If anyone asks you, you can respond this way."

16.5 Closing Prayer

One of the students says the prayer from Lesson # 3.

16.6 Teacher's Suggestion for the Week

"Dear children, please try to remember all that was said about a student of Bahá'í Children Classes. When you are at home, tell your parents this. Goodbye and see you all next class."

17. Cleanliness

"Alláh-u-Abhá class."

17.1 Opening Prayer
One of the students says the prayer from Lesson # 3.

17.2 Review Last Week's Lesson
The teacher repeats the previous week's lesson and asks children some questions.

17.3 Break: Songs, Games, Student Registration and Children's Cleanliness

Songs:
Practice the song "My Love is My Stronghold", and sing other songs the children know.

Game: "Relay Race"
Divide the children into two teams. Ask each team to form a line. Place two stones in the distance about 20 paces away. Give a stick to the first child in each line. When you say "Go!", the first child runs as fast as he can and touches the stone with the stick and runs back to give the stick to the next person in the line, who will repeat the action of the first child. The team, which finishes first, is the winner.

If there is time, the "Trees in the Garden" Play can be performed.

17.4 The Necessity of Observing Cleanliness (Being Clean)
"Dear children, today I want to talk to you again about cleanliness. I do so because there are more things about cleanliness that I have not yet mentioned and you need to know and follow them.

Remember Bahá'u'lláh and 'Abdu'l-Bahá have both emphasised to us the importance of cleanliness. Bahá'í children must be an example of cleanliness. Please listen carefully to a few more things on how to be clean.

1. Always have a clean handkerchief with you. A handkerchief can be made from a small piece of cloth. Always wipe your nose with your handkerchief. It does not look nice to pick one's nose with a finger or to clean the nose with your hands. Bahá'í children should always try to have a handkerchief.
2. Avoid breathing in dust whenever possible. Learn to breathe from your nose and not from your mouth. When you are passing through a dusty place, cover your mouth and nose with your handkerchief or something else in order to stop the dust from getting into your lungs. Dust is very harmful for your health.
3. Use soap to clean your hands. Water alone does not get rid of dirt and grease. Use soap when you want to wash your hands.
4. Always wash your hands before you eat.

Let me summarise what we have discussed today about cleanliness:

- Always have a clean handkerchief with you.
- Avoid breathing dust whenever you can.
- Cover your mouth and nose in dusty places.
- Use soap to clean your hands.
- Always wash your hands before eating.

17.5 Closing Prayer
One of the students says the prayer from Lesson # 11.

17.6 Teacher's Suggestion for the Week
"Dear children, try to be clean and neat all the time. Goodbye and see you all next class."

18. There are Bahá'ís everywhere

"Alláh-u-Abhá class."

18.1 Opening Prayer
One of the students says the prayer from Lesson # 3.

18.2 Review Last Week's Lesson
The teacher asks children questions about the previous lesson.

18.3 Break: Songs, Games, Student Registration and Children's Cleanliness

Songs:
Sing songs the children have learned.

Game: "Who Is Knocking At My Door"
One child is blindfolded and sits down on a bench, with his/her back to everyone else.   The teacher points to another child, who goes up to the child who is seated and knocks on the bench.   The child who is seated says: "Who is knocking at my door?"   The other child, trying to disguise his/her voice says: "It's me!"   The child who is seated tries to guess who is knocking. The blindfolded child has three guesses, and then it is another child's turn to be blindfolded.

18.4 There are Bahá'ís Everywhere
Discuss the subject with the students in a manner such as the one below:

"Dear children, today there are Bahá'ís everywhere in the world. They are our spiritual brothers, sisters, mothers and fathers. Some Bahá'ís live in places where it is very cold. Some Bahá'ís live in places where it is very hot. People of all colours: black, white, yellow and red, have become Bahá'ís. Every country in the world that you go to, you will find Bahá'ís. We Bahá'ís should obey the teachings of Bahá'u'lláh and love each other, as we love our family. When all the people of the world become Bahá'ís, everyone will love each other.

"We should thank God that Bahá'u'lláh has guided us to His Faith and has given us spiritual brothers and sisters everywhere. Wherever we go to see the Bahá'ís, it is as if we are among our own family and relatives. Thanks God, the Faith is everywhere.

"Dear children, you must have heard that sometimes people do not want to be friends with one another because they are of different races, different tribes or their skin is of a different colour. This is very sad. It is called prejudice and it has caused lots of suffering in the world. As Bahá'ís we must be friends with everyone, no matter where they are from.

"Now, thank God, things are getting better. More and more people are realising what Bahá'u'lláh has said us is true. People of different colours are all the same human race and all are equal in the sight of God. When we see someone who looks different from us or who is a different colour we should be happy. In a garden, it is beautiful when there are flowers of many different colours. In the same way it is nice to see people of many different colours, tribes and races coming together as friends.

"History has shown that in the United States of America, in South Africa and elsewhere, when people of different races started to become friends with each other and even to marry one another, the Bahá'ís were always amongst the first to over come these kinds of prejudice. They did this because they believed, with all their hearts, what Bahá'u'lláh has said about the different peoples of the world. Bahá'u'lláh says:

Ye are the fruits of one tree, and the leaves of one branch.[viii]

The teacher can talk about this quote, and help the children to understand and memorise it.

Note:
The teacher may use Bahá'í post-cards, books and photographs to show the children Bahá'ís from different backgrounds. This, with simple explanations about the photographs, will help children of this tender age to understand that Bahá'ís come from all over the world. The Bahá'í Faith is truly international.

18.5 Closing Prayer
One of the students says the prayer from Lesson # 11.

18.6 Teacher's Suggestion for the Week
"Dear children, there are Bahá'ís everywhere in the world. Wherever we go as Bahá'ís, we have brothers and sisters. We should therefore know the importance of being a Bahá'í, value it, and try to follow the teachings of Bahá'u'lláh in our daily lives. Goodbye and see you all next class."

19. Shoghi Effendi: The Guardian of the Bahá'í Faith

"Alláh-u-Abhá class."

19.1 Opening Prayer
One of the students says the prayer from Lesson # 3.

19.2 Review of the Previous Lesson
The teacher asks the children questions about the previous lesson.

19.3 Break: Songs, Games, Student Registration and Children's Cleanliness

Songs:
Sing songs the children have learned.

Game: "Sharing"
A car tire (or other low object) is placed on the ground. Then the children try to see how many of them can stand on it at the same time.

If desired, the "Trees in the Garden" play can be performed.

19.4 Shoghi Effendi: The Guardian of the Bahá'í Faith
Below is one way of discussing this subject with the children. (The teacher will need to have at least one of the photographs of the beloved Guardian ready in the class.)

"Dear children, this is a photograph of the beloved Guardian, Shoghi Effendi. After 'Abdu'l-Bahá passed away from this world and ascended to the next world, Shoghi Effendi became the Head of the Bahá'í Faith and the leader of all the Bahá'ís in the world.

Every Bahá'í must accept and obey, whatever Shoghi Effendi has said or written. 'Abdu'l-Bahá has told us that obeying Shoghi Effendi is like obeying God. Shoghi Effendi was the spiritual father of us all. He loved us all and worked hard all his life to educate us. He lived in Haifa, Israel, where he worked hard for the Faith. Shoghi Effendi also wrote many books and letters to educate and guide the people of the world.

"Before Bahá'u'lláh passed away from this world, He said that 'Abdu'l-Bahá should take care of the Bahá'ís after His passing. Before 'Abdu'l-Bahá passed away, He said that Shoghi Effendi should take care of the Bahá'ís after His passing. He told us to obey whatever Shoghi Effendi tells us, so that God may be happy with us. If we want God to be happy with us in this world and in the next, we should follow whatever Shoghi Effendi has told us to do. Bahá'ís from all over the world and from different backgrounds love Shoghi Effendi and try their best to obey Him.

"Shoghi Effendi loved children very much. He said parents should educate their children well, so that they will become good Bahá'ís and will serve the Faith of Bahá'u'lláh when they grow up. Shoghi Effendi is like our father. He worked hard all his life to educate us and to guide us. Blessed is the person that Shoghi Effendi is happy with. You, dear children, should try hard to make sure that Shoghi Effendi is happy with you all."

Note:
The teacher should expand on the subject in any manner thought fit until the children, based on their own understanding, grasp the importance of the station of Shoghi Effendi.

19.5 Closing Prayer
One of the students says the prayer from Lesson # 11.

19.6 Teacher's Suggestion for the Week
"Dear children, always try your best, to make sure that Shoghi Effendi is happy with you. Goodbye and see you all next class."

20. Review and expansion of the previous lesson

"Alláh-u-Abhá class."

20.1 Opening Prayer
One of the students says the prayer from Lesson # 3.

20.2 Review Last Week's Lesson (Shoghi Effendi)
The teacher repeats the previous lesson and discusses more about the beloved Guardian, Shoghi Effendi, with the children. The subject can be expanded as much as the children can understand, on what Shoghi Effendi has done for the Faith and for us. Various photographs of Shoghi Effendi should be available to show to the children.

20.3 Break: Songs, Games, Student Registration and Children's Cleanliness

Songs:
Sing songs the children have learned.

Game: "The Rhythm"
All the children sit down in a circle. Very slowly, they perform the following sequence:

1. Slap their legs once.
2. Clap their hand once.
3. Snap their fingers once.
4. Repeat the sequence several times.

When everyone has learned to carry the rhythm, let the group then call out the name of each child in turn, pronouncing the name at the moment they snap their fingers. Afterwards, let one child say everybody's name while the rhythm continues aloud. Variation:

Instead of names, each person could say a shape, colour or quality, or could count numbers.

20.4 Closing Prayer

One of the students says the prayer from Lesson # 11.

20.5 Teacher's Suggestion for the Week

"Dear children, tell your parents at home, what you have learned about Shoghi Effendi. Goodbye and see you all next class."

21. Review of Lessons # 5, 7 and 9

"Alláh-u-Abhá class."

21.1 Opening Prayer (One of the children says the prayer from Lesson # 3)

21.2 Review of Lessons from Lessons # 5, 7 and 9

21.3 Break: Songs, Games, Student Registration and Children's Cleanliness

21.4 Closing Prayer (One of the children says the prayer from Lesson # 11)

22. Review of Lessons # 10 and 12

"Alláh-u-Abhá class."

22.1   Opening Prayer (One of the children says the prayer from Lesson # 3)

22.2   Review of Lessons from Lessons # 10 and 12

22.3   Break: Songs, Games, Student Registration and Children's Cleanliness

22.4   Closing Prayer (One of the children says the prayer from Lesson # 11)

23. Review of Lessons # 13 and 17

"Alláh-u-Abhá class."

23.1   Opening Prayer (One of the children says the prayer from Lesson # 3)

23.2   Review of Lessons from Lessons # 13 and 17

23.3   Break: Songs, Games, Student Registration and Children's Cleanliness

23.4   Closing Prayer (One of the children says the prayer from Lesson # 11)

24. Review of Lessons # 18 and 19

"Alláh-u-Abhá class."

24.1   Opening Prayer (One of the children says the prayer from Lesson # 3)

24.2   Review of Lessons from Lessons # 18 and 19

24.3   Break: Songs, Games, Student Registration and Children's Cleanliness

24.4   Closing Prayer (One of the children says the prayer from Lesson # 11)

25. Preparing for End of Year 1 Celebration

"Alláh-u-Abhá class."

25.1 Opening Prayer
One of the children says the prayer from Lesson # 3.

25.2 Preparing for End of Year 1 Celebration
The teacher may explain the following about the celebration:

"Dear children, we have reached the end of the first year of your Bahá'í Education. It would be nice to celebrate it. Your parents can participate in the celebration and hear what you have learned, during this year. Now we want to prepare the programme for the celebration in which every one of you will participate."

One example of the programme for the celebration is as follows. The teacher should feel free to change it as appropriate, and may have other exciting ideas to make this a special event for the children and their families.

1. Opening Prayer (One of the children says a prayer)
2. Songs sung by the children
3. A talk by one of the students on the benefits of Bahá'í Children's Classes. The teacher will have to assist the student to prepare the talk.
4. A talk by a few of the students on the various subjects they have learned during the year. Topics such as cleanliness, kindness to animals, and obedience to one's parents, should be included. The teacher is to help in the preparation.
5. Perform "Trees in the Garden" play.
6. Sing songs

The teacher will need to explain the programme carefully to the children, so they understand what is going to happen and know the parts of the programme. The teacher should try to make sure all the children are involved and have a role to play in the programme. Some will say prayers, some will give short talks and some will perform in the play.

The children should have plenty of opportunity to practice the programme, before the actual celebration takes place. It is important that they feel familiar and comfortable with the programme so they can be excited when the time of yearend celebration comes, and not be nervous.

25.3 Break: Songs, Games, Student Registration and Children's Cleanliness

25.4 Closing Prayer
One of the children says the prayer from Day 11.

26. Year-End Celebration

The celebration is organised with the full participation of the students and the presence of their parents and some of the close family friends. Also members or representatives of the Local Spiritual Assembly, Child Education Committee and assistants to the Auxiliary Board members of the area should be invited. If there are other children's classes in the nearby communities they may also be invited.

REFERENCES

[i] **'Abdu'l-Bahá,** *Selections from the Writings of 'Abdu'l-Bahá,* p. 147

[ii] **'Abdu'l-Bahá ,** *Bahá'í Prayers* (US Edition), p. 37

[iii] **'Abdu'l-Bahá ,** *Selections from the Writings of 'Abdu'l-Bahá,* p. 159

[iv] **'Abdu'l-Bahá ,** *Selections from the Writings of 'Abdu'l-Bahá,* p. 256

[v] **'Abdu'l-Bahá ,** *Selections from the Writings of 'Abdu'l-Bahá,* p. 147

[vi] **'Abdu'l-Bahá,** *Authorised Translation*

[vii] **'Abdu'l-Bahá,** *Authorised Translation*

[viii] **Bahá'u'lláh,** *Tablets of Bahá'u'lláh,* p. 16